**Copyright
WILMOORE**

All rights reserved. No part of this publication may be reproduced, distributed, or transmitted in any form or by any means, including photocopying, recording, or other electronic or mechanical methods, without the prior written permission of the publisher, except in the case of brief quotations embodied in critical reviews and certain other noncommercial uses permitted by copyright law.

# Contents

| | |
|---|---|
| INTRODUCTION | 5 |
| Hydroponic Marijuana | 14 |
| Modern Hydroponics | 15 |
| Benefits of Hydroponics | 16 |
| TECHNIQUES | 19 |
| STATIC SOLUTION CULTURE | 20 |
| CONTINUOUS-FLOW SOLUTION CULTURE | 21 |
| AEROPONICS | 25 |
| FOGPONICS | 28 |
| PASSIVE SUB-IRRIGATION | 28 |
| EBB AND FLOW (FLOOD AND DRAIN) SUB-IRRIGATION | 30 |
| RUN-TO-WASTE | 30 |
| DEEP WATER CULTURE | 32 |
| TOP FED DEEP WATER | 34 |
| ROTARY | 35 |
| SUBSTRATES (GROWING SUPPORT MATERIALS) | 36 |
| EXPANDED CLAY AGGREGATE | 36 |
| GROWSTONES | 38 |
| COIR PEAT | 38 |
| RICE HUSKS | 39 |
| VERMICULITE | 40 |
| PUMICE | 40 |

| | |
|---|---|
| SAND | 41 |
| GRAVEL | 41 |
| WOOD FIBRE | 42 |
| SHEEP WOOL | 42 |
| ROCK WOOL | 43 |
| BRICK SHARDS | 44 |
| POLYSTYRENE PACKING PEANUTS | 45 |
| NUTRIENT SOLUTIONS | 45 |
| Organic hydroponic solutions | 48 |
| ADDITIVES | 49 |
| EQUIPMENT | 50 |
| MIXING SOLUTIONS | 52 |
| ADDITIONAL improvements | 53 |
| KEY TIPS FOR GROWING MARIJUANA USING HYDROPONICS | 54 |
| THE PROS AND CONS OF EACH METHOD | 62 |
| NUTRIENT REQUIREMENTS | 64 |
| MAKING A CHOICE | 66 |
| THESE STRAINS ARE A GREAT PLACE TO START | 67 |
| How to Grow Marijuana Hydroponically | 70 |
| Setting Up the Basics | 71 |
| Lighting and Ventilation | 74 |
| Germinating and Planting | 78 |
| Caring For Your Plant | 80 |

Harvesting and Curing ............................................................. 86
Tips for Growing Marijuana Using Hydroponics .................... 88
CONCLUSION ............................................................................ 96

## INTRODUCTION

Hydroponics is a subset of hydroculture, which is a method of growing plants without soil by instead using mineral nutrient solutions in a water solvent. Terrestrial plants may be grown with only their roots exposed to the nutritious liquid, or the roots may be physically supported by an inert medium such as perlite or gravel.The nutrients used in hydroponic systems can come from an array of different sources, including (but not limited to) from fish excrement, duck manure, or purchased chemical fertilisers. Plants commonly grown hydroponically include tomatoes, peppers, cucumbers, lettuces, and marijuana. The word hydroponics comes from the roots "hydro", meaning water, and "ponos", meaning labor, this method of gardening does not use soil.

Sounds high tech and futuristic, right? It's not.The earliest examples of hydroponics date back to the Hanging Gardens of Babylon and the Floating Gardens of China. Humans used these techniques thousands of years ago. Although the general theory behind hydroponics remains the same, modern technology has enabled us to grow plants faster, stronger, and healthier.

The earliest published work on growing terrestrial plants without soil was the 1627 book Sylva Sylvarum or 'A Natural History' by Francis Bacon, printed a year after his death. Water culture became a popular research technique after that. In 1699, John Woodward published his water culture experiments with spearmint. He found that plants in less-pure water sources grew better than plants in distilled water. By 1842, a list of nine elements believed to be essential for plant growth had been compiled, and the discoveries of German botanists Julius von Sachs and Wilhelm Knop, in the years 1859–1875, resulted in a development of the technique of soilless cultivation.Growth of terrestrial plants without soil in mineral nutrient solutions was called solution culture. It quickly became a standard research and teaching technique and is still widely used. Solution culture is, now considered, a type of hydroponics where there is no inert medium.

In 1929, William Frederick Gericke of the University of California at Berkeley began publicly promoting that solution culture be used for agricultural crop production.He first termed it aquaculture but later found that aquaculture was already applied to culture of aquatic organisms. Gericke created a sensation by growing tomato vines twenty-five feet (7.6 metres) high in his back yard in mineral nutrient solutions rather than soil.He introduced the term hydroponics, water culture, in 1937, proposed to him by W. A. Setchell, a phycologist with an extensive education in the classics. Hydroponics is derived from neologism υδρωπονικά (derived from Greek ὕδωρ=water and πονέω=cultivate), constructed in analogy to γεωπονικά (derived from Greek γαία=earth and πονέω=cultivate), geoponica, that which concerns agriculture, replacing, γεω-, earth, with ὑδρο-, water.

Reports of Gericke's work and his claims that hydroponics would revolutionize plant agriculture prompted a huge number of requests for further information. Gericke had been denied use of the University's greenhouses for his experiments due to the administration's skepticism, and when the University tried to compel him to release his preliminary nutrient recipes developed at home he requested greenhouse space and time to improve them using appropriate research facilities. While he was eventually provided greenhouse space, the University assigned Hoagland and Arnon to re-develop Gericke's formula and show it held no benefit over soil grown plant yields, a view held by Hoagland. In 1940, Gericke published the book, Complete Guide to Soil less Gardening, after leaving his academic position in a climate that was politically unfavorable.

Two other plant nutritionists, Dennis R. Hoagland and Daniel I. Arnon, at the University of California were asked to research Gericke's claims. The two wrote a classic 1938 agricultural bulletin, The Water Culture Method for Growing Plants Without Soil, which made the claim that hydroponic crop yields were no better than crop yields with good-quality soils. Crop yields were ultimately limited by factors other than mineral nutrients, especially light. This research, however, overlooked the fact that hydroponics has other advantages including the fact that the roots of the plant have constant access to oxygen and that the plants have access to as much or as little water as they need. This is important as one of the most common errors when growing is over- and under- watering; and hydroponics prevents this from occurring as large amounts of water can be made available to the plant and any water not used, drained away, recirculated, or actively aerated, eliminating anoxic conditions, which drown root systems in soil. In soil, a grower needs to be very experienced to know exactly how much water to feed the plant. Too much and the plant will be unable to access oxygen; too little and the plant will lose the ability to transport nutrients, which are typically moved into the roots while in solution. These two researchers developed several formulas for mineral nutrient solutions, known as Hoagland solution. Modified Hoagland solutions are still in use.

One of the earliest successes of hydroponics occurred on Wake Island, a rocky atoll in the Pacific Ocean used as a refueling stop for Pan American Airlines. Hydroponics was used there in the 1930s to grow vegetables for the passengers. Hydroponics was a necessity on Wake Island because there was no soil, and it was prohibitively expensive to airlift in fresh vegetables.

In the 1960s, Allen Cooper of England developed the Nutrient film technique. The Land Pavilion at Walt Disney World's EPCOT Center opened in 1982 and prominently features a variety of hydroponic techniques.

In recent decades, NASA has done extensive hydroponic research for its Controlled Ecological Life Support System (CELSS). Hydroponics research mimicking a Martian environment uses LED lighting to grow in a different color spectrum with much less heat. Ray Wheeler, a plant physiologist at Kennedy Space Center's Space Life Science Lab, believes that hydroponics will create advances within space travel, as a bioregenerative life support system.

In 2007, Eurofresh Farms in Willcox, Arizona, sold more than 200 million pounds of hydroponically grown tomatoes. Eurofresh has 318 acres (1.3 km2) under glass and represents about a third of the commercial hydroponic greenhouse area in the U.S. Eurofresh tomatoes were pesticide-free, grown in rockwool with top irrigation.

As of 2017, Canada had hundreds of acres of large-scale commercial hydroponic greenhouses, producing tomatoes, peppers and cucumbers.

Due to technological advancements within the industry and numerous economic factors, the global hydroponics market is forecast to grow from $226.45 million USD in 2016 to $724.87 million USD by 2023.

The advantage to growing hydroponically is that you deliver all the nutrients the plant needs right to its roots. In soil, the roots have to seek out and extract all nutrients, but with hydroponics, you take the work out of finding nutrients so the plant can focus more of its energy on growing bid and making flowers buds. Therefore you will end up with much faster growth and higher yields than if you grew your marijuana plants in soil.

Hydroponics can be very simple or very complex, depending on your set-up. I recommend with starting with a method that's on the simple side, and then trying a more complex method once you have a little experience under your belt.

## Hydroponic Marijuana

Let's start with the basics, so we can build a strong understanding of what it is we're talking about. The name "hydroponics" comes from the Latin language, and it translates directly to 'water working'.

This is a method of cultivating your cannabis where you grow each plant in a flow or bath of water that is both heavily enriched with healthy nutrients and highly oxygenated.

When using the hydroponic method of growing, you will not be using any soil at all to pot your plants in, and there is no sterile or inert growing medium. Every part of the nutrients and substance that your cannabis needs will be provided by the solutions in the water you use.

This sophisticated method allows the nutrients, water, and air to get to your plant directly through the roots. Due to your plant not needing any extra energy to absorb these essentials and no need for massive root webs into the soil, your marijuana grows way faster!

When cultivating the perfect crop and yield, you will have to control the entire atmosphere in your hydraulic system because of the way that the plants draw all of their nutrients from both the water and the air.

Hydraulic systems are ideal for those who are wanting to grow their marijuana in an area with minimal rainfall, and for those wanting to try an innovative and very rewarding new way of growing their plants.

## Modern Hydroponics

The earliest modern reference to hydroponics (last 100 years) was by a man named William Frederick Gericke. While working at the University of California, Berkeley, he began to popularize the idea that plants could be grown in a solution of nutrients and water instead of soil. Naturally, the general public, as well as William's colleagues, doubted this claim. He quickly proved them wrong by growing 25 foot high tomato vines using only water and nutrients.

He decided to call this growing method hydroponics. The shocking results of Gericke's experiment with tomatoes prompted further research into the field. More research was performed by University of California scientists, who uncovered a great deal of benefits related to soilless plant cultivation.

## Benefits of Hydroponics

One of the biggest advantages that hydroponics has over soil growing is water conservation. When growing plants in soil, a grower has to be very experienced to know how much water to give his plants. Too much and the plant's roots are not able to get enough oxygen. Too little and the plant can dry out and die. Hydroponics solves this problem in three different ways.

- Oxygenated Nutrient Reservoir

The water reservoir can be constantly oxygenated, making sure that the plant's roots obtain the optimum level of oxygen. Additionally, the problem of watering is solved by the fact that the plant's root system no longer has soil surrounding it, blocking oxygen uptake by the roots.

- Uses Less Water

Hydroponics uses much less water than soil farming because it can be recirculated. In traditional farming, water is poured over the ground and seeps into the soil. Only a small fraction of the water actually gets used by the plant. Hydroponics allows for the unused water to be recycled back into the reservoir, ready for use in the future. In dry and arid areas, this is a massive benefit.

- Total Growing Control

The final major benefit of hydroponics is the amount of control a grower has over the environment. Pests and diseases are much easier to deal with – your environment is often times portable and raised off of the ground. This makes it hard for bugs to reach your plants. Any soil-related diseases are completely written off in hydroponics as well. Lastly, you're able to control the amount of nutrients provided to your plant precisely, saving on nutrition costs.

- Farming of the Future

With all of these advantages, it seems as if there's nothing wrong with hydroponics! Not entirely true. Soil does act as a buffer for growing errors in hydroponics, errors are much more costly and can ruin an entire crop. In addition, higher levels of humidity do invite fungi and mildew to the system, which can ruin a crop.

In my opinion, these are small prices to pay for the vast improvements that hydroponics has over traditional growing methods. We're seeing commercial hydroponic greenhouses pop up all over the world.

In a world where fresh water and food supply are such hot issues, I see hydroponics as a major way to solve these problems in a sustainable and ecologically conscious way. The farming of the future has begun!

## TECHNIQUES

There are two main variations for each medium: sub-irrigation and top irrigation For all techniques, most hydroponic reservoirs are now built of plastic, but other materials have been used including concrete, glass, metal, vegetable solids, and wood. The containers should exclude light to prevent algae and fungal growth in the nutrient solution.

There are two main variations for each medium: sub-irrigation and top irrigation. For all techniques, most hydroponic reservoirs are now built of plastic, but other materials have been used including concrete, glass, metal, vegetable solids, and wood. The containers should exclude light to prevent algae and fungal growth in the nutrient solution.

## STATIC SOLUTION CULTURE

In static solution culture, plants are grown in containers of nutrient solution, such as glass Mason jars (typically, in-home applications), plastic buckets, tubs, or tanks. The solution is usually gently aerated but may erated. If un-aerated, the solution level is kept low enough that enough roots are above the solution so they get adequate oxygen. A hole is cut in the lid of the reservoir for each plant. A single reservoir can be dedicated to a single plant, or to various plants. Reservoir size can be increased as plant size increases. A home made system can be constructed from plastic food containers or glass canning jars with aeration provided by an aquarium pump, aquarium airline tubing and aquarium valves. Clear containers are covered with aluminium foil, butcher paper, black plastic, or other material to exclude light, thus helping to eliminate the formation of algae. The nutrient solution is changed either on a schedule, such as once per week, or when the concentration drops below a certain level as determined with an electrical conductivity meter. Whenever the solution is depleted below a certain level, either water or fresh nutrient solution is added. A Mariotte's bottle, or a float valve, can be used to automatically maintain the solution level. In raft solution culture, plants are placed in a sheet of buoyant plastic that is floated on the surface of the nutrient solution. That way, the solution level never drops below the roots.

## CONTINUOUS-FLOW SOLUTION CULTURE

In continuous-flow solution culture, the nutrient solution constantly flows past the roots. It is much easier to automate than the static solution culture because sampling and adjustments to the temperature and nutrient concentrations can be made in a large storage tank that has potential to serve thousands of plants. A popular variation is the nutrient film technique or NFT, whereby a very shallow stream of water containing all the dissolved nutrients required for plant growth is recirculated past the bare roots of plants in a watertight thick root mat, which develops in the bottom of the channel and has an upper surface that, although moist, is in the air. Subsequent to this, an abundant supply of oxygen is provided to the roots of the plants. A properly designed NFT system is based on using the right channel slope, the right flow rate, and the right channel length. The main advantage of the NFT system over other forms of hydroponics is that the plant roots are exposed to adequate supplies of water, oxygen, and nutrients. In all other forms of production, there is a conflict between the supply of these requirements, since excessive or deficient amounts of one results in an imbalance of one or both of the others. NFT, because of its design, provides a system where all three requirements for healthy plant growth can be met at the same time, provided that the simple concept of NFT is always remembered and practised. The result of these advantages is that higher yields of high-quality produce are obtained over an extended period of cropping. A downside of NFT is that it has very little buffering against interruptions in the flow (e.g., power outages). But, overall, it is probably one of the more productive techniques.[citation needed]

The same design characteristics apply to all conventional NFT systems. While slopes along channels of 1:100 have been recommended, in practice it is difficult to build a base for channels that is sufficiently true to enable nutrient films to flow without ponding in locally depressed areas. As a consequence, it is recommended that slopes of 1:30 to 1:40 are used. This allows for minor irregularities in the surface, but, even with these slopes, ponding and water logging may occur. The slope may be provided by the floor, benches or racks may hold the channels and provide the required slope. Both methods are used and depend on local requirements, often determined by the site and crop requirements.

As a general guide, flow rates for each gully should be one liter per minute. At planting, rates may be half this and the upper limit of 2 L/min appears about the maximum. Flow rates beyond these extremes are often associated with nutritional problems. Depressed growth rates of many crops have been observed when channels exceed 12 meters in length. On rapidly growing crops, tests have indicated that, while oxygen levels remain adequate, nitrogen may be depleted over the length of the gully. As a consequence, channel length should not exceed 10–15 meters. In situations where this is not possible, the reductions in growth can be eliminated by placing another nutrient feed halfway along the gully and halving the flow rates through each outlet.

## AEROPONICS

Aeroponics is a system wherein roots are continuously or discontinuously kept in an environment saturated with fine drops (a mist or aerosol) of nutrient solution. The method requires no substrate and entails growing plants with their roots suspended in a deep air or growth chamber with the roots periodically wetted with a fine mist of atomized nutrients. Excellent aeration is the main advantage of aeroponics.aeroponic techniques have proven to be commercially successful for propagation, seed germination, seed potato production, tomato production, leaf crops, and micro-greens.[20] Since inventor Richard Stoner commercialized aeroponic technology in 1983, aeroponics has been implemented as an alternative to water intensive hydroponic systems worldwide.[21] The limitation of hydroponics is the fact that 1 kilogram (2.2 lb) of water can only hold 8 milligrams (0.12 gr) of air, no matter whether aerators are utilized or not.Another distinct advantage of aeroponics over hydroponics is that any species of plants can be grown in a true aeroponic system because the microenvironment of an aeroponic can be finely controlled. The limitation of hydroponics is that certain species of plants can only survive for so long in water before they become waterlogged. The advantage of aeroponics is that suspended aeroponic plants receive 100% of the available oxygen and carbon dioxide to the roots zone, stems, and leaves,[22] thus accelerating biomass growth and reducing rooting times. NASA research has shown that aeroponically grown plants have an 80% increase in dry weight biomass (essential minerals) compared to hydroponically grown plants. Aeroponics used 65% less water than hydroponics. NASA also concluded that aeroponically grown plants require ¼ the nutrient input compared to hydroponics.[23][24] Unlike hydroponically grown plants, aeroponically grown plants will not suffer transplant shock when transplanted to soil, and offers growers the ability to reduce the spread of disease and pathogens. Aeroponics is also widely used in laboratory studies of plant physiology and plant pathology. Aeroponic techniques have been given special attention from NASA since a mist is easier to handle than a liquid in a zero-gravity environment.

## FOGPONICS

Fogponics is a derivation of aeroponics wherein the nutrient solution is aerosolized by a diaphragm vibrating at ultrasonic frequencies. Solution droplets produced by this method tend to be 5–10 μm in diameter, smaller than those produced by forcing a nutrient solution through pressurized nozzles, as in aeroponics. The smaller size of the droplets allows them to diffuse through the air more easily, and deliver nutrients to the roots without limiting their access to oxygen.

## PASSIVE SUB-IRRIGATION

Passive sub-irrigation, also known as passive hydroponics, semi-hydroponics, or hydroculture, is a method wherein plants are grown in an inert porous medium that transports water and fertilizer to the roots by capillary action from a separate reservoir as necessary, reducing labor and providing a constant supply of water to the roots. In the simplest method, the pot sits in a shallow solution of fertilizer and water or on a capillary mat saturated with nutrient solution. The various hydroponic media available, such as expanded clay and coconut husk, contain more air space than more traditional potting mixes, delivering increased oxygen to the roots, which is important in epiphytic plants such as orchids and bromeliads, whose roots are exposed to the air in nature. Additional advantages of passive hydroponics are the reduction of root rot and the additional ambient humidity provided through evaporations.

Hydroculture compared to traditional farming in terms of crops yield per area in a controlled environment was roughly 10 times more efficient than traditional farming, uses 13 times less water in one crop cycle than traditional farming, but on average uses 100 times more kilojoules per kilogram of energy than traditional farming.

## EBB AND FLOW (FLOOD AND DRAIN) SUB-IRRIGATION

In its simplest form, there is a tray above a reservoir of nutrient solution. Either the tray is filled with growing medium (clay granules being the most common) and then plant directly or place the pot over medium, stand in the tray. At regular intervals, a simple timer causes a pump to fill the upper tray with nutrient solution, after which the solution drains back down into the reservoir. This keeps the medium regularly flushed with nutrients and air. Once the upper tray fills past the drain stop, it begins recirculating the water until the timer turns the pump off, and the water in the upper tray drains back into the reservoirs.

## RUN-TO-WASTE

In a run-to-waste system, nutrient and water solution is periodically applied to the medium surface. The method was invented in Bengal in 1946; for this reason it is sometimes referred to as "The Bengal System" This method can be set up in various configurations. In its simplest form, a nutrient-and-water solution is manually applied one or more times per day to a container of inert growing media, such as rockwool, perlite, vermiculite, coco fibre, or sand. In a slightly more complex system, it is automated with a delivery pump, a timer and irrigation tubing to deliver nutrient solution with a delivery frequency that is governed by the key parameters of plant size, plant growing stage, climate, substrate, and substrate conductivity, pH, and water content.

In a commercial setting, watering frequency is multi-factorial and governed by computers or PLCs.

Commercial hydroponics production of large plants like tomatoes, cucumber, and peppers uses one form or another of run-to-waste hydroponics.

In environmentally responsible uses, the nutrient-rich waste is collected and processed through an on-site filtration system to be used many times, making the system very productive.

Some bonsai are also grown in soil-free substrates (typically consisting of akadama, grit, diatomaceous earth and other inorganic components) and have their water and nutrients provided in a run-to-waste form.

## DEEP WATER CULTURE

The hydroponic method of plant production by means of suspending the plant roots in a solution of nutrient-rich, oxygenated water. Traditional methods favor the use of plastic buckets and large containers with the plant contained in a net pot suspended from the centre of the lid and the roots suspended in the nutrient solution. The solution is oxygen saturated by an air pump combined with porous stones. With this method, the plants grow much faster because of the high amount of oxygen that the roots receive. The Kratky Method is similar to deep water culture, but uses a non-circulating water reservoir.

## TOP FED DEEP WATER

Top-fed deep water culture is a technique involving delivering highly oxygenated nutrient solution direct to the root zone of plants. While deep water culture involves the plant roots hanging down into a reservoir of nutrient solution, in top-fed deep water culture the solution is pumped from the reservoir up to the roots (top feeding). The water is released over the plant's roots and then runs back into the reservoir below in a constantly recirculating system. As with deep water culture, there is an airstone in the reservoir that pumps air into the water via a hose from outside the reservoir. The airstone helps add oxygen to the water. Both the airstone and the water pump run 24 hours a day.

The biggest advantage of top-fed deep water culture over standard deep water culture is increased growth during the first few weeks.[citation needed] With deep water culture, there is a time when the roots have not reached the water yet. With top-fed deep water culture, the roots get easy access to water from the beginning and will grow to the reservoir below much more quickly than with a deep water culture system. Once the roots have reached the reservoir below, there is not a huge advantage with top-fed deep water culture over standard deep water culture. However, due to the quicker growth in the beginning, grow time can be reduced by a few weeks.

## ROTARY

A rotary hydroponic garden is a style of commercial hydroponics created within a circular frame which rotates continuously during the entire growth cycle of whatever plant is being grown. While system specifics vary, systems typically rotate once per hour, giving a plant 24 full turns within the circle each 24-hour period. Within the center of each rotary hydroponic garden can be a high intensity grow light, designed to simulate sunlight, often with the assistance of a mechanized timer.

Each day, as the plants rotate, they are periodically watered with a hydroponic growth solution to provide all nutrients necessary for robust growth. Due to the plants continuous fight against gravity, plants typically mature much more quickly than when grown in soil or other traditional hydroponic growing systems. Due to the small foot print a rotary hydroponic system has, it allows for more plant material to be grown per square foot of floor space than other traditional hydroponic systems

## SUBSTRATES (GROWING SUPPORT MATERIALS)

One of the most obvious decisions hydroponic farmers have to make is which medium they should use. Different media are appropriate for different growing techniques.

### EXPANDED CLAY AGGREGATE

Baked clay pellets are suitable for hydroponic systems in which all nutrients are carefully controlled in water solution. The clay pellets are inert, pH-neutral, and do not contain any nutrient value.

The clay is formed into round pellets and fired in rotary kilns at 1,200 °C (2,190 °F). This causes the clay to expand, like popcorn, and become porous. It is light in weight, and does not compact over time. The shape of an individual pellet can be irregular or uniform depending on brand and manufacturing process. The manufacturers consider expanded clay to be an ecologically sustainable and re-usable growing medium because of its ability to be cleaned and sterilized, typically by washing in solutions of white vinegar, chlorine bleach, or hydrogen peroxide ($H_2O_2$), and rinsing completely.

Another view is that clay pebbles are best not re-used even when they are cleaned, due to root growth that may enter the medium. Breaking open a clay pebble after a crop has been shown to reveal this growth.

## GROWSTONES

Growstones, made from glass waste, have both more air and water retention space than perlite and peat. This aggregate holds more water than parboiled rice hulls. Growstones by volume consist of 0.5 to 5% calcium carbonate – for a standard 5.1 kg bag of Growstones that corresponds to 25.8 to 258 grams of calcium carbonate. The remainder is soda-lime glass.

## COIR PEAT

Coco peat, also known as coir or coco, is the leftover material after the fibres have been removed from the outermost shell (bolster) of the coconut. Coir is a 100% natural grow and flowering medium. Coconut coir is colonized with trichoderma fungi, which protects roots and stimulates root growth. It is extremely difficult to over-water coir due to its perfect air-to-water ratio; plant roots thrive in this environment. Coir has a high cation exchange, meaning it can store unused minerals to be released to the plant as and when it requires it. Coir is available in many forms; most common is coco peat, which has the appearance and texture of soil but contains no mineral content.

## RICE HUSKS

Parboiled rice husks (PBH) are an agricultural byproduct that would otherwise have little use. They decay over time, and allow drainage, and even retain less water than growstones. A study showed that rice husks did not affect the effects of plant growth regulators.

## PERLITE

Perlite is a volcanic rock that has been superheated into very lightweight expanded glass pebbles. It is used loose or in plastic sleeves immersed in the water. It is also used in potting soil mixes to decrease soil density. Perlite has similar properties and uses to vermiculite but, in general, holds more air and less water and is buoyant

## VERMICULITE

Like perlite, vermiculite is a mineral that has been superheated until it has expanded into light pebbles. Vermiculite holds more water than perlite and has a natural "wicking" property that can draw water and nutrients in a passive hydroponic system. If too much water and not enough air surrounds the plants roots, it is possible to gradually lower the medium's water-retention capability by mixing in increasing quantities of perlite

## PUMICE

Like perlite, pumice is a lightweight, mined volcanic rock that finds application in hydroponics.

## SAND

Sand is cheap and easily available. However, it is heavy, does not hold water very well, and it must be sterilized between uses

## GRAVEL

The same type that is used in aquariums, though any small gravel can be used, provided it is washed first. Indeed, plants growing in a typical traditional gravel filter bed, with water circulated using electric powerhead pumps, are in effect being grown using gravel hydroponics. Gravel is inexpensive, easy to keep clean, drains well and will not become waterlogged. However, it is also heavy, and, if the system does not provide continuous water, the plant roots may dry out.

## WOOD FIBRE

Wood fibre, produced from steam friction of wood, is a very efficient organic substrate for hydroponics. It has the advantage that it keeps its structure for a very long time. Wood wool (i.e. wood slivers) have been used since the earliest days of the hydroponics research.However, more recent research suggests that wood fibre may have detrimental effects on "plant growth regulators".[non-primary source needed

## SHEEP WOOL

Wool from shearing sheep is a little-used yet promising renewable growing medium. In a study comparing wool with peat slabs, coconut fibre slabs, perlite and rockwool slabs to grow cucumber plants, sheep wool had a greater air capacity of 70%, which decreased with use to a comparable 43%, and water capacity that increased from 23% to 44% with use. Using sheep wool resulted in the greatest yield out of the tested substrates, while application of a biostimulator consisting of humic acid, lactic acid and Bacillus subtilis improved yields in all substrates.

## ROCK WOOL

Rock wool (mineral wool) is the most widely used medium in hydroponics. Rock wool is an inert substrate suitable for both run-to-waste and recirculating systems. Rock wool is made from molten rock, basalt or 'slag' that is spun into bundles of single filament fibres, and bonded into a medium capable of capillary action, and is, in effect, protected from most common microbiological degradation. Rock wool is typically used only for the seedling stage, or with newly cut clones, but can remain with the plant base for its lifetime. Rock wool has many advantages and some disadvantages. The latter being the possible skin irritancy (mechanical) whilst handling (1:1000). Flushing with cold water usually brings relief. Advantages include its proven efficiency and effectiveness as a commercial hydroponic substrate. Most of the rock wool sold to date is a non-hazardous, non-carcinogenic material, falling under Note Q of the European Union Classification Packaging and Labeling Regulation (CLP).

Mineral wool products can be engineered to hold large quantities of water and air that aid root growth and nutrient uptake in hydroponics; their fibrous nature also provides a good mechanical structure to hold the plant stable. The naturally high pH of mineral wool makes them initially unsuitable to plant growth and requires "conditioning" to produce a wool with an appropriate, stable pH.

## BRICK SHARDS

Brick shards have similar properties to gravel. They have the added disadvantages of possibly altering the pH and requiring extra cleaning before reuse

## POLYSTYRENE PACKING PEANUTS

Polystyrene packing peanuts are inexpensive, readily available, and have excellent drainage. However, they can be too lightweight for some uses. They are used mainly in closed-tube systems. Note that non-biodegradable polystyrene peanuts must be used; biodegradable packing peanuts will decompose into a sludge. Plants may absorb styrene and pass it to their consumers; this is a possible health risk.

## NUTRIENT SOLUTIONS

The formulation of hydroponic solutions is an application of plant nutrition, with nutrient deficiency symptoms mirroring those found in traditional soil based agriculture. However, the underlying chemistry of hydroponic solutions can differ from soil chemistry in many significant ways. Important differences include:

Unlike soil, hydroponic nutrient solutions do not have cation-exchange capacity (CEC) from clay particles or organic matter. The absence of CEC means the pH and nutrient concentrations can change much more rapidly in hydroponic setups than is possible in soil.

Selective absorption of nutrients by plants often imbalances the amount of counterions in solution. This imbalance can rapidly affect solution pH and the ability of plants to absorb nutrients of similar ionic charge. For instance, nitrate anions are often consumed rapidly by plants to form proteins, leaving an excess of cations in solution. This cation imbalance can lead to deficiency symptoms in other cation based nutrients (e.g. $Mg^{2+}$) even when an ideal quantity of those nutrients are dissolved in the solution.

Depending on the pH and/or on the presence of water contaminants, nutrients such as iron can precipitate from the solution and become unavailable to plants.

Routine adjustments to pH, buffering the solution, and/or the use of chelating agents is often necessary.

As in conventional agriculture, nutrients should be adjusted to satisfy Liebig's law of the minimum for each specific plant variety.nevertheless, generally acceptable concentrations for nutrient solutions exist, with minimum and maximum concentration ranges for most plants being somewhat similar. Most nutrient solutions are mixed to have concentrations between 1,000 and 2,500 ppm.acceptable concentrations for the individual nutrient ions, which comprise that total ppm figure, are summarized in the following table. For essential nutrients, concentrations below these ranges often lead to nutrient deficiencies while exceeding these ranges can lead to nutrient toxicity. Optimum nutrition concentrations for plant varieties are found empirically by experience and/or by plant tissue tests.

The formulation of hydroponic solutions is an application of plant nutrition, with nutrient deficiency symptoms mirroring those found in traditional soil based agriculture. However, the underlying chemistry of hydroponic solutions can differ from soil chemistry in many significant ways. Important differences include:

## Organic hydroponic solutions

Organic fertilizers can be used to supplement or entirely replace the inorganic compounds used in conventional hydroponic solutions. However, using organic fertilizers introduces a number of challenges that are not easily resolved. Examples include: organic fertilizers are highly variable in their nutritional compositions. Even similar materials can differ significantly based on their source (e.g. the quality of manure varies based on an animal's diet).

organic fertilizers are often sourced from animal byproducts, making disease transmission a serious concern for plants grown for human consumption or animal forage.organic fertilizers are often particulate and can clog substrates or other growing equipment. Sieving and/or milling the organic materials to fine dusts is often necessary.

some organic materials (i.e. particularly manures and offal) can further degrade to emit foul odors.

## ADDITIVES

In addition to chelating agents, humic acids can be added to increase nutrient uptake

Managing nutrient concentrations and pH values within acceptable ranges is essential for successful hydroponic horticulture. Common tools used to manage hydroponic solutions include:

Electrical conductivity meters, a tool which estimates nutrient ppm by measuring how well a solution transmits an electric current.

pH meter, a tool that uses an electric current to determine the concentration of hydrogen ions in solution.

Litmus paper, disposable pH indicator strips that determine hydrogen ion concentrations by color changing chemical reaction.

Graduated cylinders or measuring spoons to measure out premixed, commercial hydroponic solutions.

## EQUIPMENT

Chemical equipment can also be used to perform accurate chemical analyses of nutrient solutions. Examples include: Balances for accurately measuring materials.

Laboratory glassware, such as burettes and pipettes, for performing titrations. Colorimeters for solution tests which apply the Beer–Lambert law.

Using chemical equipment for hydroponic solutions can be beneficial to growers of any background because nutrient solutions are often reusable. Because nutrient solutions are virtually never completely depleted, and should never be due to the unacceptably low osmotic pressure that would result, re-fortification of old solutions with new nutrients can save growers money and can control point source pollution, a common source for the eutrophication of nearby lakes and streams.

Although pre-mixed concentrated nutrient solutions are generally purchased from commercial nutrient manufacturers by hydroponic hobbyists and small commercial growers, several tools exist to help anyone prepare their own solutions without extensive knowledge about chemistry. The free and open source tools HydroBuddy and HydroCal have been created by professional chemists to help any hydroponics grower prepare their own nutrient solutions. The first program is available for Windows, Mac and Linux while the second one can be used through a simple JavaScript interface. Both programs allow for basic nutrient solution preparation although HydroBuddy provides added functionality to use and save custom substances, save formulations and predict electrical conductivity values. There is also a small robotic helper available called Eddy, created by the Flux Farm.It can send various information such as pH level, temperature, relative humidity, and contamination directly to its designed smartphone app and can even propose some simple solutions to any detected problems

## MIXING SOLUTIONS

Often mixing hydroponic solutions using individual salts is impractical for hobbyists and/or small-scale commercial growers because commercial products are available at reasonable prices. However, even when buying commercial products, multi-component fertilizers are popular. Often these products are bought as three part formulas which emphasize certain nutritional roles. For example, solutions for vegetative growth (i.e. high in nitrogen), flowering (i.e. high in potassium and phosphorus), and micronutrient solutions (i.e. with trace minerals) are popular. The timing and application of these multi-part fertilizers should coincide with a plant's growth stage. For example, at the end of an annual plant's life cycle, a plant should be restricted from high nitrogen fertilizers. In most plants, nitrogen restriction inhibits vegetative growth and helps induce flowering

## ADDITIONAL improvements
- Growrooms

With pest problems reduced and nutrients constantly fed to the roots, productivity in hydroponics is high; however, growers can further increase yield by manipulating a plant's environment by constructing sophisticated growrooms.

- CO2 enrichment

Carbon dioxide § Agricultural and biological applications

To increase yield further, some sealed greenhouses inject CO2 into their environment to help improve growth and plant fertility.

## KEY TIPS FOR GROWING MARIJUANA USING HYDROPONICS

The cliché, "an ounce of prevention equals a pound of cure" may well be overused, but it is still a good measure to use when growing marijuana. If enough attention to detail is taken during the setup phase of a hydroponic grow operation, then the chances for a successful crop are greatly increased.

The precise course of action taken will depend on your unique space and resources, and of course any unique needs of the particular strain of cannabis that you are growing. All that aside, there are still some tasks and practices that should be observed in any hydroponic growing area to keep your plants as healthy and productive as possible.Start with sterile tanks and equipment- If you can afford to buy all new equipment to start your growing operations, this step may not be necessary at first, but eventually all tanks, reservoirs, pipes, filters and any other physical part of your hydro system will need to be sanitized to prevent the development and spread of pathogens, especially root rots. Plan on having several bottles of isopropyl alcohol and hydrogen peroxide on hand to disinfect your equipment on a regular basis.

Make sure you start with clean, pH neutral water- Ideally the water circulating through your hydroponic system is at a pH of 7. If not, a reverse osmosis (RO) system will create and provide neutral water. Distilled water can be used as well until an RO system can be obtained.Watch your temperatures- Ideally the water flowing through your system will be about 65 F (18 C) to facilitate good nutrient absorption and to prevent the buildup of algae. The air temperature, however can be warmer. If you can achieve about 75 F (24 C) in your grow room, your marijuana plants should be quite content. Maintain proper humidity levels- Cannabis plants do best in varying levels of humidity based on their stage of development. When your "girls" are young, they need to have humidity levels in the 60-70 percent range. As they develop and move into the blooming phase, they only need about 40 percent humidity. This can be best achieved with a humidifier and dehumidifier used accordingly. Attain proper lighting- There are numerous types of grow lights out there and champions and critics of all. The right types of grow light for your setup will depend on your space, the distance between your lights and your plants and your budget. High Intensity Discharge (HID) lights are better for larger grow rooms with good airflow and ventilation. Compact Fluorescent lights (CFL) are better for smaller rooms. Light from Light Emitting Diode (LED) fixtures is good for small grow areas, but is more costly than the CFLs. Whichever type is selected, make sure that it can produce light in sufficient amounts between 400 and 700 nanometers. A relatively inexpensive light meter can help to determine if your grow lights are getting the job done.

- Maintain proper ventilation/air flow- Keeping the air moving around is critical for plant health and aids in even temperature distribution. Fans should be mounted or placed so that they can cover the most area unobstructed. Proper ventilation will help to maintain appropriate air temperatures if it gets too hot, but will also help with air exchange.


- Understand pH- Fortunately this is not difficult and there are meters that can take pH readings. This is important because if the pH of your water is not in the proper range, your plants will not grow well or may even die. For hydroponic cannabis, aim for a pH of about 6.0, but allow for a range between high 5s and low 6s. Understand EC readings- Electrical conductivity (EC) is a measure of the total dissolved solids (TDS) in your hydroponic water. Like with pH, there are many effective meters on the market and there are many that take both readings (pH and EC). The EC level will tell you how rich in nutrients your circulating water is. If the EC is too low, your plants aren't getting enough; if it's too high, you can "burn" your plants with too high of a nutrient level. The EC for hydroponically grown cannabis will fluctuate depending on the stage of growth. As seedlings or clones are first put into a system, the EC levels should be less than 1.3 and can be as low as .5 for clones. When they start to grow however, expect to maintain an EC level that continually climbs toward 2.0. When your plants finally reach the flowering phase, they may need an EC up to almost 2.5 depending on the strain grown. Check your EC levels often. The closer you can maintain proper EC, the more productive your cannabis plants will be.

- Find a reliable seed source- All of the planning, preparation and procuring of necessary products can't make cannabis of poor genetics into a robust strain. A cannabis plant can only produce what it is genetically predisposed to produce. Improving its growing environment and attending to its needs ensures that it will come as close to this potential as possible.
- Keep good records - You cannot improve what you cannot measure. Even the best growers have bad crops and sometimes novices get lucky. To remove as much of the "luck" factor and to focus on results, keep track of everything. The more detailed notes you keep on temperatures, planting dates, EC levels, pH levels, humidity

levels and any other factor that you can measure, will allow you to make informed decisions going forward to make continual improvements or to maintain high yields.

As you probably know, soil is the green part of our "blue planet." Although it only dominates 30% of the Earth's surface, it's where most plants grow and have done so for millions of years. Because of this, soil has accumulated minerals and organic matter that is very hard to replicate with any other method. That is why a lot of traditional cannabis aficionados will only grow and/or buy cannabis that is cultivated outdoors in soil. But it's still important to note that most soil growers will add nutrient solutions or nutrient-rich materials like earthworm castings and manure to enhance their medium.

Hydroponic, on the other hand, takes away all the unpredictability of soil. The term hydroponic is now very commonly used for all mediums other than soil. Water-based growing operations without a stationary medium are referred to as "solution culture." Because of this, we'll be defining hydroponics as methods where the roots of the plant are in constant contact with a water solution. Nutrients are then added in liquid form to the water, creating a new solution. This will consist of only the absolute essentials for the plant and will give the grower much more control over the end result.

## THE PROS AND CONS OF EACH METHOD

What differentiates these two methods is mainly a matter of yield vs quality. Growing outdoors with a soil medium will generally allow for much higher yields. Outside, there is no height limitation and with soil, the roots can grow and branch out freely. With proper care, a soil medium can help you grow plants that are 2m tall, offering more than 400g of quality bud per plant. Using hydroponic methods in an indoor operation won't allow for cannabis this tall. Therefore, yields won't be as high because the roots are limited by the size and volume of your coco coir, mesh pot, water bucket, grow room, etc.

Quality works in the opposite way. It's much easier to control an indoor hydroponic plantation. You'll be giving the plant the exact nutrients it needs under the perfect lighting conditions in an environment with the ideal humidity. This will also allow you to automate most of the growing process.

Soil is not as controllable. When growing cannabis outside, there will be temperature changes, uncontrollable wind, and even humidity variations. These are hard to predict and impossible to master. One can only adapt to the outside environment and hope for the best. Soil also contains organic matter and bacteria that might not be too favourable for your plant's health. These will be hard to identify until visual changes manifest on the plant.

You'll have to base your decision on finding the best combination of quantity and quality for your situation. Soil is a much more familiar medium than hydroponics and is more advisable for first time growers. There is a lot of information out there. Conduct further research to make a more informed decision.

## NUTRIENT REQUIREMENTS

When growing a complex plant like cannabis, changing the medium will affect its requirements. You'll have to adapt nutrient feeds so you're not left with an unwanted deficiency. This is a very common problem in cannabis plants that a lot of growers don't know how to deal with. Making sure your products are the appropriate ones and your pH is ideal will go a long way in preventing deficiencies or nutrient lockout.

Whether in the form of mineral powder or dissolved in water, macronutrient products will have three basic elements: nitrogen, phosphorus, and potassium. These nutrients are summarised by the N-P-K ratio composed of three numbers on the front of a nutrient bottle. Each value represents the percentage by volume of the corresponding nutrient in the solution.

In a soil medium, manure can be added, which is a nutrient-rich material. This is something that a hydroponic solution can't replicate. Soil is filled with microbes that help turn organic material like guano and worm castings into usable nutrients for your plant. In hydroponics, you'll have to feed your plants the full quantity of micro and macronutrients. Independently of the quality of your soil, you'll likely need extra supplements in order to obtain the best results. This is where the hydroponic system differentiates mostly from a soil-based medium.

Micronutrients like iron, copper, and magnesium are widely available in most soil mediums. Therefore, hydro solutions must contain more of these to compensate. They also require more nitrogen, a macronutrient abundant in soil, but not as much in water sources. This is why hydro nutrients during the vegetative stage have a higher percentage.

## MAKING A CHOICE

This is the part where you'll have to decide what to do next; which materials to buy and how much area to dedicate to your plantation. Let's recap on what we explored above.

Growing in soil will be the best choice for you if you want to keep the natural essence of the plant. You might prefer the flavour outdoor soil gives the flowers. Only consider soil if you have access to high-quality soil mediums. Soil growing is perhaps the best option if you're not growing full-time. Soil will require much less of your attention as it will be doing the bulk of the work for you.

On the other hand, if you're looking for the highest cannabinoid presence, hydroponic will be your choice. This is where you'll get those deliciously frosty 28% THC buds. It is also smart to choose hydroponics if you want an automated system. You won't be able to fully automate the process, but with methods like drip irrigation, it will reduce your chores. This will be the best method to try out if you're experienced, but have never tried it before. It's always positive to learn how cannabis grows and behaves under different conditions. You'll probably achieve better results growing hydroponically, assuming you know what you're doing.

Remember that the best choice will be the one you make. You'll make it work whether you're experienced or not. It's the motivation and passion you have that will ultimately determine your success. Even though people have been growing cannabis for thousands of years, only recently has real research gone into it. Perhaps you'll be the one to figure out the next trick or hack for growing the best cannabis flower. Go out there and experiment; just have fun!

## THESE STRAINS ARE A GREAT PLACE TO START

Whether you choose soil or hydroponics, both are capable of producing top-quality cannabis. However, if you are not sure which strain to start with, we have a beginner-friendly suggestion for both methods.

- SOIL

Soil is the traditional growing medium that has served growers for centuries. As we have alluded to though, soil can be a little tricky to manage, especially if it is your first time cultivating cannabis. With that in mind, we have picked a strain that is more forgiving than others to offset any small mistakes.

- SOMANGO XL

This flavoursome beauty benefits from indica-dominant genetics, and can be harvested in as little as nine weeks. Not only is that less time for things to go wrong, but Somango XL is considered ideal for both newbie and experienced growers. Her hardiness allows simple mistakes like nutrient fluctuation to occur without significant repercussions

## How to Grow Marijuana Hydroponically

Whether you call it weed, cannabis, pot, marijuana, or something else, the plant known as Cannabis sativa is actually easy to grow at home when you know what you need to do. Growing hydroponically will provide you with higher yields and a shorter grow time compared to growing in soil, but it can often be difficult for the beginning grower to get started with hydroponics. However, most people think of plants growing in water when they think "hydroponics" but actually your plants will get many of the benefits of hydroponics as long as they're getting their nutrients directly in their water supply. However because of superior air to water ratio in hydroponics, it remains the industry standard. This tutorial will show you step-by-step how to grow your marijuana in 3-4 months using the (arguably) easiest hydroponic method: hand-watering in a soil-less medium.

## Setting Up the Basics

- If you haven't already yet, consider growing marijuana the traditional way before you grow hydro. Growing hydroponic marijuana is a bit more difficult than growing marijuana in soil: You're optimizing for nutrients, light, and ventilation, which can be hard if you've never grown marijuana before.[1] Don't necessarily expect to jump straight from 0 to 60 without a hitch. Although growing is easy if you have the right knowledge and information, it usually takes time to gather both of those things.

On the other hand, other constraints may force your hand and compel you to start off growing hydro. If you're a first-time grower and want to try hydro, know that you can be successful. Do your research but avoid telling your friends or acquaintances. Nothing can get you shut down quicker than blabbering about your hydro unit.

Consider growing other plants hydroponically in addition to marijuana. Growing hydro doesn't need to mean just growing weed. You can grow lettuce, tomatoes, or even mushrooms hydroponically. Experimenting with these crops first may teach you valuable lessons you can use when growing marijuana.

- Obtain all the necessary items. If you're careful to shop around, you should be able to get everything you need for five plants for $300-$500. You should expect to get 1-3 ounces off each plant at the end. You will need (see the Things You'll Need section below for further details):
  - Marijuana seeds or clones
  - White paint or mylar
  - Hydroponic nutrients
  - Pots

- Potting medium such as coco coir
- Compact fluorescent lights (CFLs)
- A timer
- pH soil test

* Prep your walls. Plants grow with the aid of light. If you're growing indoors, this presents somewhat of a problem. Many grow rooms are housed in dark spaces where light is absorbed instead of reflected. To get the most bang for your buck and to make the best possible weed you'll want your walls to either be painted a glossy white or be covered with mylar.

* Painting your walls a semi-gloss or flat white is probably the simplest solution. The flatter the white, the better, as glossy white reflects roughly 55% of the light coming from your source.

Titanium white might be your best bet if you do decide to paint.

- Mylar is highly reflective. It has a reflection rate of roughly 90%, making it a much more efficient coating material than something like aluminum foil. But because mylar reflects light and heat very efficiently, you'll need to be sure that you have proper ventilation in your grow room.

## Lighting and Ventilation

- Set up your grow lights. They should start out a little higher than the height of your pots, and should have room to be raised to the final height of your plants. There are a million ways to set up or hang the lights and you will need to do what works for your grow area. The simplest method is to either hang them from the bar in your closet or you can also clamp the lights onto something nearby that is the right height.

- Clamp reflectors are great for using CFLs. The socket is already attached, no wiring or electrical work is really needed, and the housing helps to reflect as much light as possible. Remember that any excess light that doesn't hit your plants is wasted light.

- Make sure your lights are producing at least the minimum, and preferably the ideal, amount of lumens per square foot. Lumens is a unit for the total amount of visible light emitted by a source. Therefore, it's helpful to talk about how many lumens a source emits, as well as how many lumens your growing operation needs. On an average day, the sun emits about 5,000 to 10,000 lumens per square foot. The absolute minimum needed to grow average-sized plants is around 3,000 lumens per square foot. Note that the actual amount of lumens that reach the bottom of your plant will fluctuate depending on the distance of the light source and the reflectivity of the surroundings.

The ideal amount for a standard grow operation is somewhere between 7,000 and 10,000 lumens per square foot.

To figure out how many lumens per square foot you're working with, simply divide the total lumens by the total square feet. Say you're working with two 300-watt CFLs — each with 40,000 lumens — in a 3' x 3' x 2' area. Your total lumens is 80,000 and your total footage is 18'. 80,000 ÷ 18 ≈ 4,400 lumens per square foot.

- Take care that you don't burn or overheat your plants with your light source. Having sufficient light will help your marijuana grow tall, healthy, and chronic. But what to do about overheating. The ideal temperature for your grow operation is somewhere between 80 °F (27 °C) and 85 °F (29 °C), with 90 °F (32 °C) being the max.[6] If your temperature is anywhere below this, consider adding a small heater to generate additional heat. If your temperature is anywhere above this, a fan and additional ventilation may need to be added to help provide the perfect growing conditions.

- Get your grow room ventilated. Proper ventilation is absolutely necessary for vibrant plants. If your grow room is in a closet, for example, there's not much more that you can do other than an oscillating fan. In a box, however, adding a duct system is efficient for many home growers. To make a duct system, a simple squirrel cage fan (it looks like a hamster wheel) attached to 6" ducts will help mitigate rising temperatures and pungent odors.

As with any operation, including an additional oscillating fan will help strengthen the stalks of the marijuana plants as they grow.

## Germinating and Planting

- Germinate your marijuana seed. To get your weed seed to sprout, simply wet a large paper towel and lightly wrap your seeds in between the paper towel. Place the paper towel and cover with another plate to make sure the paper towel doesn't dry out. Alternately, place the damp paper towel in a sealable plastic bag and rest somewhere dark and warm for at least 24 hours.

- Once the seed has germinated, transfer to a rock wool block. Rock wool is a great medium to grow the early-stage marijuana plant in. Once the seedling has started sprouting a significant root system, you can transfer the plant into the coco coir.

- Start feeding your plants with water (filtered or tap) mixed with nutrients. Adjust the water to have a pH of 5.5 to 6.0 for best results.

In the beginning, give your plants nutrients at quarter strength and work your way up to full strength nutrients over the course of a week or two. One of the biggest mistakes many new growers make is giving their plant too many nutrients which can hurt your plant. Most brands of nutrients will come with a hydroponic feeding schedule which can usually be followed exactly.

You can get Fox Farms Hydroponic Nutrient Trio and follow their included instructions exactly if you're not sure what to get for nutrients. The Fox Farms

Hydroponic Nutrient Trio works great for growing marijuana. After you have added your nutrients to your water, you'll want to adjust the pH of the solution to around 5.5-6.0 to ensure proper nutrient absorption.

### Caring For Your Plant

- Water your plants with pH'ed and nutrient-filled water whenever the top of the coco coir starts feeling dry. This will start out with you watering the plants every couple of days when they're small, and may end up with you watering them once a day towards the end of the plant's flowering cycle.

- Ensure that at least a little extra run-off water comes out the bottom of the container whenever you water your plants to ensure that unused nutrients don't build up in your medium. Coco coir and perlite are very forgiving if you accidentally over or under-water your plant, but make sure to adjust your watering schedule accordingly if you notice your plant's leaves are wilting or drooping.

- Keep your marijuana plants in the vegetative stage of growth until they are about half their final desired height. You can keep your marijuana plants in the vegetative stage by giving them 18-24 hours of light a day.

Your marijuana has two major grow phases after it's a seedling, the vegetative and flowering stages. You will treat the plant differently depending on what stage it's in. During the vegetative stage, your marijuana plants are only worried about growing and getting big. In order to keep your plants in the vegetative stage, they will need to get at least 18 hours of light a day. This simulates "summer," when the days are long. You can give your plants as much as 24 hours of light per day during the vegetative stage, but you'll find success as long as you stay within that 18-24 hours or light per day range.

The height of the plant is often the main factor when determining how long to keep your marijuana plants in the vegetative stage. Your plant can double its height in the flowering stage, so you will want to keep the plant in the vegetative stage until it's about half it's desired final height. If growing in a closet, it's a good idea to keep your plants in the vegetative stage until they're 6-18" tall.

- Start the flowering stage when your plants achieved the correct height. Tell your cannabis plants to begin the flowering stage by changing to a 12 hours of light/12 hours of darkness schedule so that they start producing buds. This simulates the beginning of fall and winter.

In the flowering stage, your plants stop worrying about growing as much, and start putting their energy into growing flowers/buds. You will need to tell your plants when it's time to start flowering. In the wild, marijuana plants start flowering when the days start getting shorter because that's a sign that winter is coming. In order to simulate the same conditions, you will need to switch your light schedule so that your lights are on for 12 hours a day, and off for 12 hours a day.

- Sex your plants and get rid of any males. Determine the gender of your plants 1 to 2 weeks after first changing the lights for the flowering stage. Get rid of any males you happen to find in the bunch. Males will pollinate females, causing females to start diverting energy from THC production into seed growth. Pollinated weed isn't unsmokable, but it's a lot less potent than unpollinated weed and picking out seeds can be a pain.

After making the switch in light schedule, you will start noticing the first signs of your plant's gender about 1-2 weeks. Female plants will grow white hairs and males will start growing grape-like balls that eventually become pollen sacs. In order to maximize on the amount of bud you get, you will want to make sure you remove any male plants so they don't pollinate your females. If male and female plants stay together, than your females will end up making lots of seeds instead of buds. You also don't get any usable bud off of a male plant, only pollen.

- Wait patiently while your plants mature in the flowering stage. This is often the toughest part for beginning growers. The Flowering Stage can last from 6 weeks to 12 weeks or longer depending on the marijuana strain that you're growing with.

- Start feeding your marijuana plants just plain, pH'ed water 1-2 weeks before it's time to harvest. Otherwise, you may actually be able to taste the nutrients in your final buds (your marijuana could have a chemical after-taste). This process is typically known as a flush.

Towards the end of your plant's flowering cycle, you may notice that some of the oldest leaves start turning yellow and falling off. This is totally normal and is a sign that your plant is taking nitrogen out of the leaves and putting them into the buds/flowers. This is a signal that it's getting close to harvest time, and you'll usually want to stop giving your plants nutrients with their water for the last 1-2 weeks to ensure the best possible taste of your final bud.

## Harvesting and Curing

- Harvest your plants when they're ready by cutting down the whole plant or cutting off pieces of buds at a time. There are many methods to determine the right time to harvest your plant. Basically, you want to harvest when 50-75% of the white pistils/hairs have turned amber/brown. Another way to tell is when the trichomes (also known as crystals or resin glands) are either all white/milky or half white and half amber.

Harvesting earlier will give a more thoughtful or in-your-head marijuana experience while harvesting later will give you a heavier or more relaxing marijuana experience. You will want to experiment to find what harvest time is the best for you.

- Trim your plant so that there aren't any leaves sticking out from the buds. Leaves will make your final smoke a lot more harsh and don't contain much THC, so you don't want them in your final product. You can still use them to make hash, butter, or Green Dragon.

- Hang your trimmed buds upside down in a cool, dark place and let them dry until the buds snap off cleanly (as opposed to just bending) when you put pressure on them.

- Place the buds in an air-tight container and leave them in a cool, dark place for 2 weeks to a month or more to "cure." Open the jar once a day to get some air ventilation and make sure you release any moisture. Moisture is your enemy when curing and will cause mold, so make sure your buds are properly dried before curing them.

**Tips for Growing Marijuana Using Hydroponics**

The cliché, "an ounce of prevention equals a pound of cure" may well be overused, but it is still a good measure to use when growing marijuana. If enough attention to detail is taken during the setup phase of a hydroponic grow operation, then the chances for a successful crop are greatly increased.

- The precise course of action taken will depend on your unique space and resources, and of course any unique needs of the particular strain of cannabis that you are growing. All that aside, there are still some tasks and practices that should be observed in any hydroponic growing area to keep your plants as healthy and productive as possible.

- Start with sterile tanks and equipment- If you can afford to buy all new equipment to start your growing operations, this step may not be necessary at first, but eventually all tanks, reservoirs, pipes, filters and any other physical part of your hydro system will need to be sanitized to prevent the development and spread of pathogens, especially root rots. Plan on having several bottles of isopropyl alcohol and hydrogen peroxide on hand to disinfect your equipment on a regular basis.

- Make sure you start with clean, pH neutral water- Ideally the water circulating through your hydroponic system is at a pH of 7. If not, a reverse osmosis (RO) system will create and provide neutral water. Distilled water can be used as well until an RO system can be obtained.

- Watch your temperatures- Ideally the water flowing through your system will be about 65 F (18 C) to facilitate good nutrient absorption and to prevent the buildup of algae. The air temperature, however can be warmer. If you can achieve about 75 F (24 C) in your grow room, your marijuana plants should be quite content.

- Maintain proper humidity levels- Cannabis plants do best in varying levels of humidity based on their stage of development. When your "girls" are young, they need to have humidity levels in the 60-70 percent range. As they develop and move into the blooming phase, they only need about 40 percent humidity. This can be best achieved with a humidifier and dehumidifier used accordingly.

- Attain proper lighting- There are numerous types of grow lights out there and champions and critics of all. The right types of grow light for your setup will depend on your space, the distance between your lights and your plants and your budget. High Intensity Discharge (HID) lights are better for larger grow rooms with good airflow and ventilation. Compact Fluorescent lights (CFL) are better for smaller rooms. Light from Light Emitting Diode (LED) fixtures is good for small grow areas, but is more costly than the CFLs. Whichever type is selected, make sure that it can produce light in sufficient amounts between 400 and 700 nanometers. A relatively inexpensive light meter can help to determine if your grow lights are getting the job done.

- Maintain proper ventilation/air flow- Keeping the air moving around is critical for plant health and aids in even temperature distribution. Fans should be mounted or placed so that they can cover the most area unobstructed. Proper ventilation will help to maintain appropriate air temperatures if it gets too hot, but will also help with air exchange.

- Understand pH- Fortunately this is not difficult and there are meters that can take pH readings. This is important because if the pH of your water is not in the proper range, your plants will not grow well or may even die. For hydroponic cannabis, aim for a pH of about 6.0, but allow for a range between high 5s and low 6s.

- Understand EC readings- Electrical conductivity (EC) is a measure of the total dissolved solids (TDS) in your hydroponic water. Like with pH, there are many effective meters on the market and there are many that take both readings (pH and EC). The EC level will tell you how rich in nutrients your circulating water is. If the EC is too low, your plants aren't getting enough; if it's too high, you can "burn" your plants with too high of a nutrient level. The EC for hydroponically grown cannabis will fluctuate depending on the stage of growth. As seedlings or clones are first put into a system, the EC levels should be less than 1.3 and can be as low as .5 for clones. When they start to grow however, expect to maintain an EC level that continually climbs toward 2.0. When your plants finally reach the flowering phase, they may need an EC up to almost 2.5 depending on the strain grown. Check your EC levels often. The closer you can maintain proper EC, the more productive your cannabis plants will be.

- Find a reliable seed source- All of the planning, preparation and procuring of necessary products can't make cannabis of poor genetics into a robust strain. A cannabis plant can only produce what it is genetically predisposed to produce. Improving its growing environment and attending to its needs ensures that it will come as close to this potential as possible.


- Keep good records - You cannot improve what you cannot measure. Even the best growers have bad crops and sometimes novices get lucky. To remove as much of the "luck" factor and to focus on results, keep track of everything. The more detailed notes you keep on temperatures, planting dates, EC levels, pH levels, humidity levels and any other factor that you can measure, will allow you to make informed decisions going forward to make continual improvements or to maintain high yields.

## CONCLUSION

Get hydroponics right, and it allows for some genuinely monstrous results. With complete control over everything your cannabis needs, managing the height of your towering beauty can become a real struggle. Our recommended strain for hydroponic growers takes this into account, without impacting yields or flavour.Treat this "sickly sweet" lady right, and she will return the devotion with 20–25% THC. In hydroponics, the growth potential of a strain is a serious consideration. Wedding Gelato is ideal because she only reaches 60–100cm in height. The precision of hydroponics allows all of her efforts to go into developing dense, THC laden buds, rather than growing out of control

CPSIA information can be obtained
at www.ICGtesting.com
Printed in the USA
LVHW080034020322
712389LV00014B/724